D0574482

Careers without College

Correction Officer

by Susan Clinton

Content Consultant:
Gabriella Daily
Director for Communications and Publications
American Correctional Association

CAPSTONE BOOKS
an imprint of Capstone Press
Mankato, Minnesota

Capstone Books are published by Capstone Press
151 Good Counsel Drive, P.O. Box 669, Mankato, Minnesota 56002
http://www.capstone-press.com

Printed in the United States of America.

Library of Congress Cataloging-in Publication Data
Clinton, Susan.
Correction officer/by Susan Clinton.
p.cm.--(Careers without college)
Includes bibliographical references (p.45) and index.
Summary: Outlines the educational requirements, duties, salary, employment outlook, and possible future positions of corrections officers.
ISBN 1-56065-700-6 (alk.paper)
1. Corrections--vocational guidance--United States--Juvenile literature. 2. Vocational guidance. [1. Corrections--Vocational guidance.] I. Title. II. Series: Careers without college (Mankato, Minn.)
HV9471.C59 1998
365'.025'73--DC21

97-35240
CIP
AC

Photo Credits:
Steve C. Healey, 36
International Stock/Bill Stanton, 4, 11
Leslie O'Shaughnessy, 17, 19, 20, 22, 25, 27 , 28, 32, 39, 41
Photo Network, cover; Dennis MacDonald, 6, 30
James L. Shaffer, 43
Unicorn Stock Photos/A. Ramey, 12, 14, 35
Kevin Vandivier, 9, 44

Table of Contents

NEW YORK

Fast Facts

Career Title	Correction Officer
Minimum Educational Requirement	High school diploma
Certification Requirement	None
U.S. Salary Range	$12,400 to $50,000
Canadian Salary Range	$20,400 to $61,300 (Canadian dollars)
U.S. Job Outlook	Much faster than the average
Canadian Job Outlook	Much faster than the average
DOT Cluster (Dictionary of Occupational Titles)	Service occupations
DOT Number	372.667-018
GOE Number (Guide for Occupational Exploration)	04.01.01
NOC (National Occupational Classification—Canada)	6462

EXIT
MICHIGAN SHERIFF
ST. CLAIR

Chapter 1

Job Responsibilities

Correction officers guard people who are in jail or prison. A correction officer's first duty is to keep the public safe from criminals. Correction officers keep prisoners from escaping.

There are two kinds of prisoners. The first kind is a person in custody. Custody means to be arrested by the police. The police question people who are in custody. The police decide if these people should be charged with crimes. If charged,

Correction officers guard people who are in jail or prison.

people stay in jail during their trials. A judge or jury decides if each person is guilty or innocent.

Criminals are the second kind of prisoners. These people are serving sentences. A sentence is time spent in a prison or correctional facility as punishment for a crime.

Working Inside the Prison

Some correction officers work in prison cell blocks. Prisoners live in small rooms called cells. Cells have locks and bars. A cell block is an area with a number of cells. Two correction officers usually guard 50 to 100 inmates.

Cell blocks can be hot and noisy. Prisoners talk and shout. Radios and televisions play loudly. Correction officers must stay alert. They must keep track of inmates to be sure the inmates do not escape. Officers count prisoners many times every day.

Sometimes correction officers search cells. They check all the doors and windows. They make sure locks and security gates work. They

Correction officers make sure locks and security gates work.

look for hidden weapons. They take away contraband. Contraband is items that are not allowed in prisons. Contraband can be weapons, drugs, ropes, or sharp tools.

Correction officers must also guard prisoners when guests visit the prisoners. Officers make sure visitors do not bring in any contraband.

Working Outside the Prison

Some officers work sentry duty. Sentry duty is work outdoors guarding prison walls. Correction officers on sentry duty often stand in towers with rifles. They try to prevent escapes. A prison needs officers on sentry duty at all times.

Correction officers may work in calmer areas. Some guard gates. They follow strict safety rules. Other officers watch prisoners on television screens. They send in other correction officers if they see trouble.

Sometimes prisoners must go to court or to a hospital. Correction officers must get prisoners

Correction officers on sentry duty stand in towers with rifles.

BANDA
PITUFOS Show
COCULA GRO.

safely out of jail or prison and back. Correction officers who travel with prisoners are patrol conductors. These officers also guard prisoners in hospitals or courtrooms.

Some correction officers guard illegal immigrants. An immigrant is a person who enters one country from another country. These correction officers are immigration officers. Immigration officers who work for the Immigration and Naturalization Service (INS) hold immigrants in custody. They check the backgrounds of the immigrants. Immigration officers send many illegal immigrants back to their home countries. They allow some immigrants to stay in the United States.

Some correction officers guard illegal immigrants.

Chapter 2

What the Job Is Like

Correction officers direct the activities of prisoners. Officers keep order in the prison. They make sure prisoners do not escape. Correction officers also help keep the prisoners safe.

Helping Prisoners Every Day

Correction officers tell new inmates the rules of the prison. They may help inmates adjust to life

Prisoners are under guard while they work, eat, bathe, and sleep.

in prison. Prisoners are never alone. They are under guard while they work, eat, bathe, and sleep.

Prisoners depend on correction officers for many things. Correction officers make sure prisoners get their meals. They send sick prisoners to prison doctors. They check cells for dirty or unsafe conditions. Correction officers pass out mail to prisoners. Correction officers also take inmates outdoors to exercise.

Correction officers give work assignments to prisoners. They watch how the inmates do their work. Prisoners can use the skills they learn after they leave the prison. Correction officers also let prisoners go to classes, to worship, or to prison libraries.

Sometimes correction officers give prisoners advice. Some officers help prisoners get ready for their release. The officers can help prisoners find jobs and places to live outside of prison. But many prisoners dislike correction officers. For this reason, correction officers must always watch out for their own safety.

Correction officers pass out mail to prisoners.

A-1

Keeping Prisons Safe

Prisons are rough places. Some inmates commit crimes inside prisons. Correction officers investigate these crimes. They may also serve as witnesses during trials.

Correction officers protect prisoners from each other. People in prisons are likely to fight. Many prisons have problems with gangs. Correction officers have to know about gangs. They have to know which prisoners belong to which gangs. Members of one gang may attack members of other gangs. Officers keep some inmates away from each other to prevent fights. At times, correction officers may have to use force.

Correction officers keep daily records. They report to their supervisors every day. Supervisors are people who manage a number of workers. Reports may be spoken or written. Officers report on prisoners' behavior. They report trouble or fights. They also warn other officers about bad situations.

Correction officers investigate crimes inmates commit inside prisons.

POLICE

VEHICLE
Radius of Curve
R
Center of mass
Acceleration
A·Cosθ
Force of Friction
W
N

Chapter 3

Training

All correction officers must be at least 18 years old. They must be at least 21 years old for many jobs. There are no training jobs for anyone younger than 18. Most correction officer jobs also require a high school degree. Correction officers cannot have arrest records.

Requirements

People who apply for correction officer jobs must usually pass written tests. Correction officers

People applying for correction officer jobs must usually pass written tests.

9:00
Civil Service
Exam
OFFICER
WEST

work in city, county, state, and federal prisons. They also work in private prisons. Each type of prison has its own requirements for correction officer jobs.

Sometimes people who want to be correction officers must take psychological examinations. Psychological means related to the mind. These tests help prison officials decide which people are best-suited to become correction officers.

Some correction officer jobs are civil service jobs. Civil service jobs are government jobs. People applying for civil service jobs must take a civil service examination. People who want federal prison jobs take these tests. The government hires the people who earn the highest test scores.

Education

Many prison officials prefer to hire correction officers who have attended college. People must complete two years of college to work in a federal prison. Some two-year colleges offer

People applying for government jobs must take a civil service test.

degrees in correctional science. A degree is a title given by a college for completing a course of study. Students learn about crime and the court system in correctional science courses. They learn how to handle prisoners. Students also study human behavior and how society works.

Correction officers can learn about the effects of drugs in health courses. Correction officers must understand the signs of drug use. They must know the effects of withdrawing from drugs. Many prisoners have drug problems. Some prisoners sneak drugs into prison.

Courses in government and communications are also helpful for correction officers. Correction officers need to know about the law and human rights. They must be able to explain things clearly. They must give written and spoken reports. Practice in writing and public speaking helps. Knowing a foreign language can also help in this job. Some prisoners do not speak English well.

Correction officers learn how to handle prisoners.

PROPERTY
OF
HUDSON
POLICE DEPT.

Many prison officials hire people who have served at least two years in the military. These people might not have college degrees. But their military experience helps them know how to deal with risky situations.

Job Training

All new correction officers go through training. Some states have special schools where their correction officers receive training. This training usually lasts four to eight weeks. New officers in federal prisons start with a three-week basic training program.

New officers learn about self-defense and the use of weapons in these training programs. They learn how to control prisoners. They also learn about prison rules and prisoners' rights. Trainees learn how to handle fires, fights, and medical problems.

These programs are only the start of a correction officer's training. New correction officers go through on-the-job training. They work

In training programs, new officers learn about self-defense and the use of weapons.

StairMaster 4000PT

with experienced officers. The experienced officers teach trainees how to perform their jobs. This training may be short and informal in small prisons. Training lasts as long as two years in other prisons.

Many jobs require officers to take training programs every year. This training teaches correction officers about new ideas and methods. Sometimes the training includes practice at shooting ranges.

Preparing Now

People who are interested in becoming correction officers can do many things to prepare for the job. Getting into good shape is one way of preparing.

Regular exercise or playing sports keeps the body in good condition. Learning self-defense skills is also valuable. Correction officers must be in good health. They must pass a health exam to get jobs.

Correction officers must be in good health.

Chapter 4

Salary and Job Outlook

In the United States, the average salary for a new correction officer is $18,400 per year. Salaries go up with more experience. The average salary for all officers is $23,000. Salaries are different in different parts of the country. New correction officers in New Jersey earn twice the salary of those in Kentucky.

Correction officers in federal prisons earn more than officers in state, county, or city

Correction officers in federal prisons earn more than officers in state, county, or city prisons.

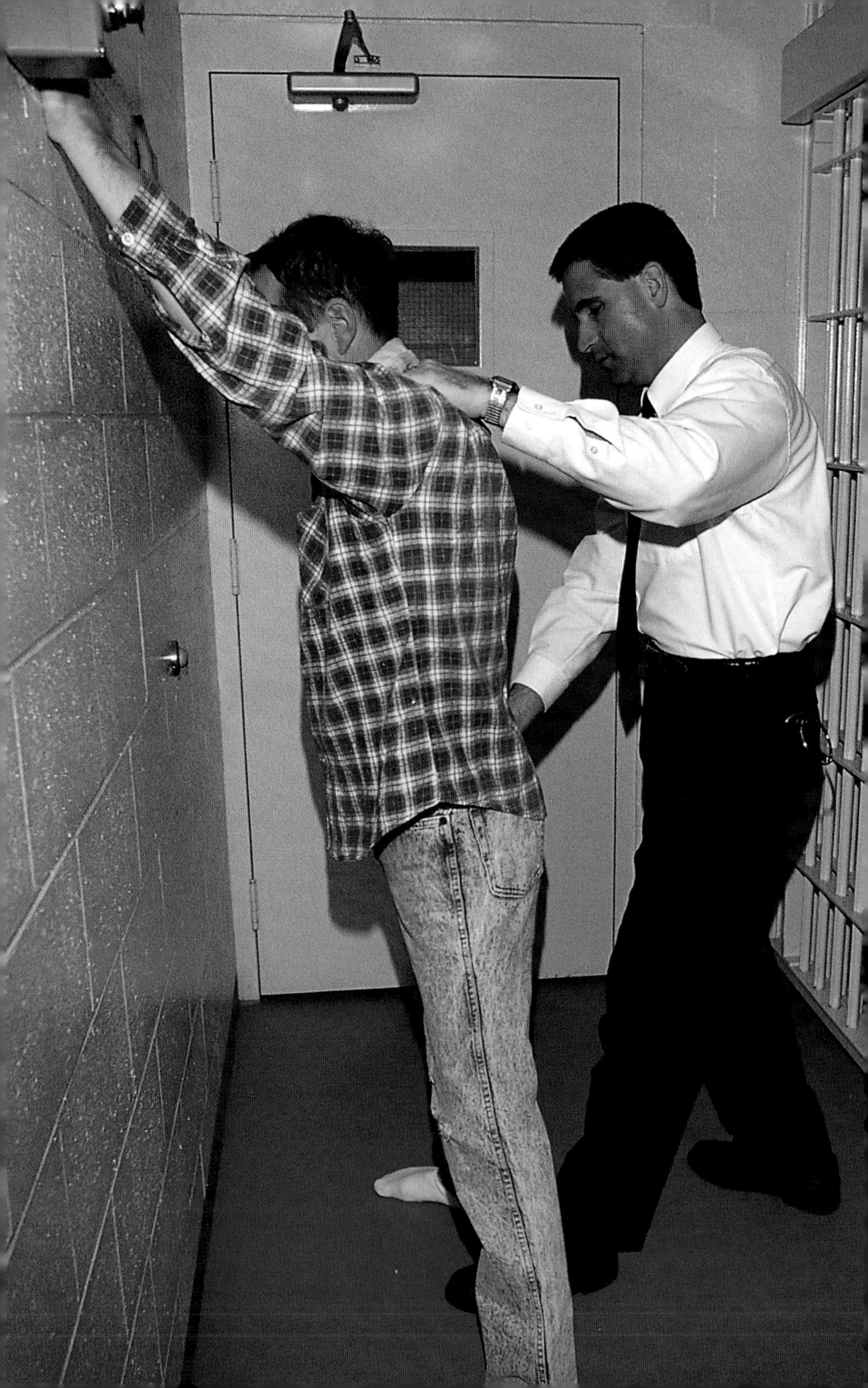

prisons. A new federal correction officer makes from $21,000 to $28,000 per year. But only three out of every 100 officers have jobs in federal prisons. Most jobs are in state prisons, city jails, or county jails.

Benefits

Prisons must have correction officers working at all times. Officers work eight-hour shifts, five days per week. Some of these eight-hour shifts may be at night or on weekends. Officers may earn extra pay for working holidays or overtime. Overtime is working more than 40 hours per week. Officers may have to work overtime during emergencies. An emergency is a sudden and dangerous situation.

Officers must always be alert for trouble. Prisoners may threaten, hurt, or even kill correction officers. This risk causes a great deal of worry and pressure. Most prisons offer health insurance for officers. Health insurance is payment of medical costs. Many health

Officers must be alert for trouble all the time.

insurance plans pay for doctors who help officers deal with pressure.

Most officers have pension plans. Pensions are payments to older people who have retired. Some jobs offer early retirement plans after a certain number of years on the job. Some civil service workers can retire at age 50. Correction officers receive payment for sick days and vacation time.

Correction officers usually receive uniforms. Sometimes correction officers live in homes that belong to the government.

Job Outlook

The number of people in prison is growing. Older prisons are crowded. The government is building many new prisons. This means the number of jobs for correction officers is increasing. Crowded prisons need more officers to watch prisoners. New prisons need new staff members. There will be a strong demand for new correction officers in the future. Because of this, good correction officers can count on keeping their jobs.

The government is building many new prisons.

Chapter 5

Where the Job Can Lead

Correction officers can work for promotions. A promotion is a move to a better job. Officers may receive promotions after they gain experience. They may also receive promotions for doing good work. Officers who receive promotions usually need more training.

Correction officers can become correction sergeants.

Kinds of Promotions

Officers may receive promotions to correction sergeant. Correction sergeants supervise correction officers. The starting salary for a correction sergeant is about $28,000 per year.

There are fewer chances for promotions in smaller jails and prisons. Correction officers can move from sergeant to higher ranks in larger prisons. Promotions bring more duties such as supervising others and managing prisons. Some correction sergeants receive promotions to warden or prison superintendent. The warden or prison superintendent is the person in charge of the prison.

Related Fields

Correction officers also move into other fields. Some correction officers move into police work. Some work as parole officers. Parole officers keep track of prisoners who are released from prison.

Promotions bring duties such as supervising others and managing prisons.

People on parole are free after serving their sentences. But they must not commit any more crimes. Parole officers try to make sure the people on parole do not commit crimes. Parole officers try to help people on parole fit into the community. They may help these people find jobs or housing.

Correction officers are important members of the community. They work to keep communities safe. Their job is to protect the people inside of prisons and the people outside of prisons. The job is hard and risky. But every community needs correction officers.

Correction officers are important members of the community.

POLICE

Words to Know

cell (SEL)—a small room with locks and bars
civil service (SIV-il SUR-viss)—jobs working for the government
contraband (KON-tra-band)—items that are not allowed in prisons
custody (KUHSS-tuh-dee)—arrested by the police
degree (di-GREE)—a title given by a college for completing a course of study
emergency (i-MUR-juhn-see)—a sudden and dangerous situation
psychological (sye-kuh-LOJ-uh-kuhl)—relating to the mind
sentence (SEN-tuhnss)—time spent in prison or a correctional facility as punishment for a crime
sentry duty (SEN-tree DOO-tee)—work outdoors guarding prison walls

POLICE
POLICE

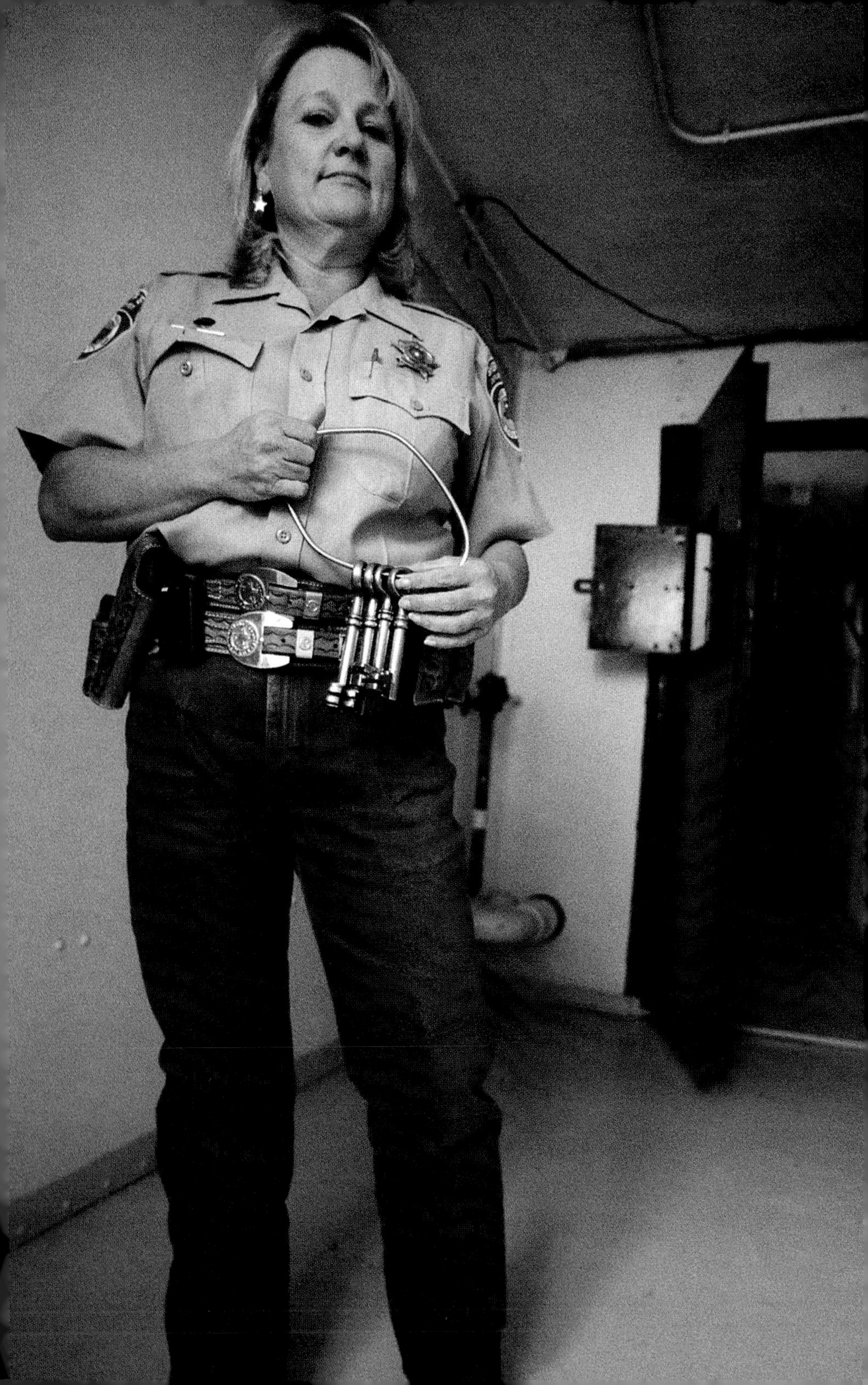

To Learn More

A Career as a Correction Officer. Chicago: Institute for Research, 1994.

Preparing for a Career in Public Safety. What Can I Do Now? Chicago: Ferguson Publishing, 1998.

Steinberg, Eve. *Correction Officer.* New York: Macmillan USA, 1997.

Stinchcomb, James. *Opportunities in Law Enforcement and Criminal Justice Careers.* Lincolnwood, Ill.: VGM Career Horizons, 1996.

Useful Addresses

American Correctional Association
4380 Forbes Boulevard
Lanham, MD 20706

The American Probation and Parole Association
c/o Council of State Governments
Iron Works Pike
PO Box 11910
Lexington, KY 40578

The International Association of Correctional Officers
Box 53
1333 South Wabash Avenue
Chicago, IL 60605

Internet Sites

COAO Directory
http://www.mgl.ca/~sroberts/dir.htm

ACA Home Page
http://www.corrections.com/aca

The Cell House
http://www.geocities.com/CapitolHill/4815/

Corrections Industry directory and guide
http://www.prisons.com

The Corrections Connection
http://www.corrections.com

Index